LIFE SPEAKS...
What Is It Saying To You?

A. R. JOHNSON

LIFE SPEAKS...
What Is It Saying To You?
Copyright © A. R. Johnson

The scripture quotations utilized in this manuscript, unless otherwise indicated, are taken from the Spirit-Filled Life Bible Copyright 1991, by Thomas Nelson, Inc.; The Holy Bible, New King James Version Copyright 1982, by Thomas Nelson, Inc.; and the New King James Bible, New Testament Copyright 1979, by Thomas Nelson, Inc. Also, The Holy Bible, Authorized King James Version, Ultra Thin Reference Edition Cornerstone Bible Publishers Copyright 1999, by Holman Bible Publishers. Used by permission. All rights reserved.

Library of Congress Control Number: 2024944019
Paperback: 979-8-89306-075-1
eBook: 979-8-89306-076-8

Printed in the United States of America

Contents

Season 1 (Spring) v

Season 2 (Summer) vii

Season 3 (Autumn) ix

Season 4 (Winter) xi

Changing Lives.. 1

"Dina" 3

Called to Duty 5

Elijah - Man of Fire 7

Be Obedient to the Lord... 9

Deep Recesses of Your Mind 11

Character... 13

Come Together 15

A Picture of Love... 17

Be My Valentine 19

SEASON 1 (SPRING)
Author's Prelude

Reflection: (S)piritual Poetry

The reflection during this season is on poems of a spiritual nature. Two terms come to mind regarding the spiritual; solemn and solace. The word solemn is described as sacred or formal. You will sense this as you read the poems covered throughout this representation of the spring season. Solace is defined as a comfort or consolation. These poems should be a source of refuge for you; a place for you to allow your mind to escape some of the harsh realities of life.

In this spiritual poetry, there is a peaceful and tranquil sentiment that transcends the natural realm. Reading these poems bears a refreshingly invigorating feeling. Place your mind at ease as you read this material. You should gain moments of peace as you reflect while reading. Likewise, ease of any tension is what you should receive. So, kick back, relax, and let yourself go as you read the poetry covered in this season of this book. I believe you will enjoy it. *–Adrian*

Life Speaks... : What Is It Saying To You?

SEASON 2 (SUMMER)
Author's Prelude

Reflection: (O)pen (Heart & Mind) Poetry

A flair for creativity is a necessary element for this season of the book. Surprise is a key factor in a suspense novel; however, with poetry the creative juices flow a little more smoothly when one has some idea of the topic of poetry they will be inclined to. Intellectual acumen allows the mind to branch out a little further when reflecting on the poetry of this summer season.

Summertime brings refreshment and an opportunity for openness of mind. The warmth in the air relays a magnificent aura that will captivate the mind as this material is read. The flow is surreal; once started, it will be difficult to stop reading the poems introduced in this open venue. *–Adrian*

Life Speaks... : What Is It Saying To You?

SEASON 3 (AUTUMN)
Author's Prelude

Reflection: I(N)timate Poetry

The "N" in iNtimate poetry is what this season is all about. This is the in thing—the cuddling that takes place between a young couple before they become man and wife. The warmth of summer is fading away. Cool briskness of autumn is headed your way. Heat generated from our bodies begins to fill the air. Time is of the essence, no need to spare.

Nuptial comes to mind when reflecting on the "N" in intimate. In this intimacy is created the special bond that could be no greater defined than that which exists between a man and his wife. From the sleigh bells that ring in the winter through the church bells that ring after an autumn wedding, nuptials take place after a union between a boy and a girl becomes solidified by their strong and pervasive love for one another.

When reading the poems of this autumn season, one cannot help but become ingratiated with the sensations associated with newfound love. The words seem to leap off of the page as you become mesmerized by the content and where the text is taking you to.   This poetry should bring an excitement from which one can indulge. *–Adrian*

Life Speaks... : What Is It Saying To You?

SEASON 4 (WINTER)
Author's Prelude

Reflection: (G)roup (Family) Poetry

Picture this—being encamped round about a sparkling fireplace with your group or family, roasting marshmallows and singing lullabies. In the cold of winter, the family or group element is the strongest bond that can be formed to fit this particular occasion. Winter sometimes brings extremely cold temperatures, but the love found in groups (families, friends, associations) trumps that brought on by weather patterns.

To maximize the effectiveness of this season, the warmth created from these poems is buttressed by their realism. During the winter season, experience coming together as a group or a whole. Sense yourselves pulling together to wrap up the old year and to start the new year afresh. Lastly, regarding the dynamic attained by these poems of several individuals comprising a group, resolve in your mind to do better in your group in the coming year and close out your winter strong. *–Adrian*

Life Speaks... : What Is It Saying To You?

Changing Lives

Every good deed turned extends a hand to another
for no stone goes unturned
If you give, something will be given in return
you don't have to question it; your time will come

Everyone has a start date and at some time there will be an end
but the things that matter most are those that are done from within…your heart

Plant a seed, but start today
for you will reap fruit along the way
It does not matter how great or how small
everyone with purpose will answer the call

Your life is a mirror and every day that you live
shows someone your example and shoes for them to fill
Are your shoes ones that someone would want to fill?

Everyone should ask themselves that question and not be afraid
for most have done wrongful things for which they were forbade
Don't look back or think if I could start all over again
just act right now and produce a lifestyle change

All of us can do better; let no one deceive you

the life we live should be for others; Mother Theresa and Dr. Martin Luther King knew

We were not created to act exactly the same way…but

we can get on the same sheet of music and blend in perfect harmony

This kind of act starts with one person at a time

so don't give up on the action; fall right into line

For life begins to crash one day at a time;

you can also begin to build, but your thoughts you must align

Take the time, please start now

We want our earth greener, but our character we must avow

If I could help a neighbor, I would do it now

Will you help me if I offered to show you how?

If you need time to think, then you need to think again

Time on this earth is not always our friend

People are hurting all over the world

When you help change the life of someone else, you help to change your own

Written by:

A.R. Johnson

"Diva"

Ever since I first laid eyes on you
you've been the most beautiful woman I've know

That illustrious glare that streams from your eyes
a beauty that's all your own

Your hands are like the petals of a rose
so elegant and gentle to the touch

Your feet are smooth like the back of a dove
cute as can be they're both soft and plush

The character you possess is strong
the very depth of your mind is sound

Every time I kiss you it tastes like wine
each time you smile it's absolutely profound

A. R. Johnson

My God, how I admire your gorgeous eyes
and the fullness of your hair is so fine

But the one thing I love about you the most
is the fact that you will always be mine

Written by:

A.R. Johnson

Called to Duty

Fix bayonets, prepare to enter the fight
Surprise attack awaits over the hill

Perdition lurks for those not skilled
Retreat is for the faint, build up your might

Tomorrow is not promised, today is at stake
Our neighbors produce on every side

Teamwork is the endeavor our hearts seek after
Duty is never limited; it's a call that you make

Introspection is key, relevance a factor
What's your plot if your future you will not seek after?

This noble deed is a call for all mankind
Stand up and strong and make up your mind

In the end what do you have if a story it does not tell?
For every man endures fright and his own private hell

A. R. Johnson

When you dawn the uniform for the very last time
Having answered the call of duty for God and man

Your understanding will now be enlightened
For you truly answered the noblest deed of mankind

Written by:

A.R. Johnson

Elijah – Man of Fire

Full of vigor, born for esteem
Not a statuesque young man, but powerful before the Lord
Calmness abounds you, humility builds your might
your words are few, but have the strength to draw a sword

Humble in spirit, grand in deed
focused on high, prayer always at your side
Able to carry on continually the mission before you,
God forever remains your guarantee

Elijah—you are man and spirit
draw your might from your spirit
Recognize your inner being
then your true character will shine freely

Can you account for every minute?
give your whole day to the Lord
Only He can fully sustain you
focusing on your every need

My prayer is that your life

every day God will guide

For every tear that I had cried

brought Jesus closely to your side

Life is not over; it is only just beginning

have no fear there is work to be done

Conquest came in the days of the prophet…

Elijah—Man of Fire

 grab your sword for there's a fight to be won

Written by:

A.R. Johnson

Be Obedient to the Lord

To be obedient to the Lord
is the least of what I can afford
To be together and of one accord
the sentiment ornately stated all across the board

If your words ring loudly as they fill the sky
and your argument becomes dominant, are you better than I?
Nay I say, for the two shall become one flesh
when we put our thoughts together and do not settle for less

"Deep calleth unto deep,"1 'tis a communication for mankind
but how does it register when it enters the mind
Will we forever be lost, tossed by the waves of the sea
for a thought is an enigma, lost in the annals of eternity

Are we afraid to go deep because it will reveal just who we are?
it is through those shallow waters by which one will never go far
To escape the judgments of man is not truly a part of life
it compares to experiencing fullness, but never loving your wife

When faced with the depth of life's complexities
there is a voice that hovers across the seven seas
His message is clear, "sharper than any two-edged sword"2
our time is now, just be obedient to the Lord

Written by:

A.R. Johnson

Deep Recesses of Your Mind

In the deep recesses of your mind
is all the truth you'll ever find

To look ahead and not behind
when all of God's words will fall in line

In the deep recesses of your mind

Jesus is "the way, the truth, and the life"3
the direct route to end all strife

The path that leads to eternal victory
just pray to Him and you will see

In the deep recesses of your mind

Continue to pray and the devil must flee
because of the price Jesus paid on the tree

A. R. Johnson

Faith is what you hold on to when you feel you're going blind
as God's love for you lurks in the deep recesses of your mind

In the deep recesses of your mind

Written by:

A.R. Johnson

Character

There are going to be good days and bad days

but how we align ourselves to see

Becomes the determinant to our character development

and helps to preserve our dignity

Society exists all around us

our environment and surroundings we chose not

But our deeply hidden values

must be the thick of any plot

If the effort we give cannot direct or change

the life of one in need

We must examine the character we possess

for in this life we lead

Every breath we take must contain the passion

and show that we're all called to plant a seed

Written by:

A.R. Johnson

Come Together

A single unit marches in stride
not always synchronized but follows a plan
Their leader develops with the help of the group
the mindset is strong; the group is at its peak

Devastation occurs—does the group fall apart
one says, now is not the time to conquer the hill
Regroup at once! What is the game plan?
to come together is an act of will

If not today, then when will the day come?
gather all of your friends
Make a declaration before the council
no moment will ever seem quite like the present

Aspiration piles high
demolition draws nigh
A dilemma unfolds
Come together—finish the fight

Life Speaks... : What Is It Saying To You?

Morality is on edge
what is the right decision to make?
The answer lies before you
come together and complete your objective

Written by:

A.R. Johnson

A Picture of Love

A beautiful smile, a glowing heart
gives a life filled with trials its brand new start

Four quarts of longsuffering and a bushel of love
is a mixture of Godliness as is seen from above

There is no one more deserving
of whom this is written to

For your life is a picture of love
and every word is true

Let God's creation bear witness
coming from both near and far

Here stands a flower which blossoms all year around
and that flower is what you are

Written by:
A.R. Johnson